Richard Pipes

THREE "WHYS" OF THE RUSSIAN REVOLUTION

Richard Pipes, Baird Professor of History at Harvard University, is the author of numerous books and essays on Russia, past and present. In 1981–82 he served as President Reagan's National Security Council adviser on Soviet and East European affairs, and he has twice received a Guggenheim fellowship. He lives in Cambridge, Massachusetts.

THREE "WHYS" OF THE RUSSIAN REVOLUTION

THREE "WHYS" OF THE RUSSIAN REVOLUTION

Richard Pipes

VINTAGE BOOKS

A Division of Random House, Inc.

New York

FIRST VINTAGE BOOKS EDITION, JUNE 1997

Library of Congress Cataloging-in-Publication Data

Pipes, Richard.
Three whys of the Russian Revolution / Richard Pipes.
p. cm.
Originally published: Toronto: Vintage Canada, 1996.
"Vintage original."
ISBN 0-679-77646-X
1. Soviet Union—History—Revolution, 1917–1921.
2. Soviet Union—History— Revolution, 1917–1921—Causes.
I. Title.
DK265.P4744 1997
947.084'1— dc21   96-46857
CIP

Vintage ISBN: 978-0-679-77646-8

Random House Web address: http://www.randomhouse.com/

Printed in the United States of America

TABLE OF CONTENTS

THREE "WHYS" OF THE
RUSSIAN REVOLUTION

INTRODUCTION

THE HISTORY OF THE RUSSIAN REVOLUTION has been my lifelong professional occupation: my first book was devoted to this subject and so was the latest, published forty years later. The various works that I brought out in the interval also dealt mostly either with the Revolution or its antecedents. My interest in this subject is in good measure explainable by the fact that I was born shortly after the Revolution in Poland, a country bordering on Russia, and have lived ever since in a world heavily influenced by the Revolution's aftereffects.

My principal histories of this momentous event are *The Russian Revolution*, published in 1990, and *Russia under the Bolshevik Regime*, brought out four years later. The two books, numbering 1,350 pages of text, cover in considerable detail Russian history from 1899 to 1924. They furnish the evidence for the generalizations made in the present volume, which is based on lectures that I gave in January 1995 at the Institute for Human Sciences in Vienna. In these lectures I addressed myself to what appear to me the three central problems of the Russian Revolution: the reasons for the collapse of tsarism, for the triumph of the Bolsheviks, and for the ascendancy of Stalin. My answers to these questions differ in many respects from those provided by the so-called "revisionist" school of historiography which has emerged in the West in the 1960s and today holds sway in academe. Whereas the revisionists, like one-time Soviet historians, stress social forces, my emphasis is on politics. The methodological disparity results in very different interpretations: in the eyes of the revisionists, events are driven by unstoppable and anonymous forces; in my eyes, the decisive factor is human will.

As my work progressed, I was able to gain access to Soviet archives. The present volume reflects information that I have acquired since the completion of work on *Russia under the Bolshevik Regime*, including that drawn from Lenin's secret depository at the Central Party Archive in Moscow.

                                        Richard Pipes

did tsarism fall? Why did the Bolsheviks gain power? Why did Stalin succeed Lenin?

Some aspects of the Russian Revolution are still shrouded in mystery, in good measure because, for some seventy-odd years, the authorities in charge of Soviet archives have closed them to foreigners as well as to independent Russian scholars. Access was given only to specialists licensed by the Communist Party and willing to uphold strictly its version of events, which centred on the proposition that the revolution was inevitable, and just as inevitably led to the Bolshevik triumph. These archival depositories, with some exceptions (notably the so-called Presidential Archive), have now been thrown open to all interested parties, making it possible for the first time to obtain a politically unbiased picture of events. I have paid several visits to the most important of these archival depositories, previously known as the Central Party Archive of the Marx–Engels–Lenin Institute, now renamed the Russian Centre for the Preservation and Study of Documents of Recent History. This archive houses the original papers of all the leading figures of what used to be known as the Marxist–Leninist movement and its subsidiaries, such as the Communist International. Although I did not find any startling revelations — ultimately the intentions of the Soviet regime, as those of any other government, are revealed by its actions — much that concerns its leaders' mentality and personal relations, previously treated as a state secret, has been illuminated by these newly released documents.

The closing of the archives to independent scholarship, however, was not the only reason for much of the prevailing misunderstanding of the Russian Revolution. The principal cause is the fact that the Soviet regime claimed to derive its political legitimacy from history, and hence treated history as a matter of high political priority. Although paying lip-service to the most perfect ideals of democracy, it never subjected itself to a popular vote. True, it did participate in the elections to the Constituent Assembly held in November 1917, but after Lenin's party, then already in power, gained less than a quarter of the votes, Lenin ordered the assembly dissolved. Subsequently no further elections, in any meaningful sense of the word, were held in the Soviet state. The Communists asserted that they had been chosen by history to accomplish mankind's momentous transition from a class-based society to a classless one. For this reason, the manner in which modern Russian history was presented and taught was to them of much greater importance than it is to societies whose legitimacy rests on a popular mandate. All Russian history, but particularly that of modern times, was completely dominated by the party's ideological organs, which tailored the facts and interpretations to suit the current party line. Thus, history was a branch of propaganda. Soviet historical literature had little to do with what actually happened, reflecting instead what the Establishment wanted people to believe had happened. Over time, the thicket of half-truths, quarter-truths, and outright lies grew so dense that the independent historian had to hack his way through it as would a traveller in an unexplored tropical forest. It is no wonder that the field of modern Russian history in the Soviet Union attracted few talented people, and none with a broad vision, since it was the exclusive preserve of the Communist Party.

Unfortunately, from the 1960s onwards, much of this thinking has also permeated Western scholarship, giving rise to the so-called "Revisionist" school whose adherents in the United States, England, and Germany, for diverse intellectual and personal reasons, came of their own free will to echo the interpretation of the Russian Revolution that was mandatory in the Soviet Union. Their "revisionism" sought to displace the independent findings of Russian émigré scholars and their Western disciples of the previous generation by adopting, with minor modifications, the themes and interpretations of Soviet post-Stalinist party-dominated pseudo-scholarship. In some cases, those who embraced revisionism did so because they genuinely came to doubt the soundness of the traditional Western approach, with its emphasis on politics. In part under the influence of Marxism and in part inspired by the French *Annales* school, they insisted on studying history "from below," or according to the premise that history is driven by social conflicts. Others who took this path had less admirable personal motives: adhering, in broad terms, to the authorized Soviet version gave them access to secondary Soviet archives and gained them such other benefits as Moscow had in its power to bestow. Also important is the fact that revisionism is built into modern intellectual life, which puts a premium on discovery and invention. Ambitious young scholars are impelled to take issue with their elders — for if they merely agree with those who have gone before, how can they make their mark? In this prevailing atmosphere, saying or doing something new is more richly rewarded than being right.

All these factors played their part, and I am not able to single out any one of them as decisive. The fact is that, if the mainstream Western scholars writing on the history of the Third Reich have been and remain unambiguously hostile to Nazism, the majority of those writing for the past thirty years about communism and the Soviet Union have been in varying degrees sympathetic to it. They have been inclined to stress the positive achievements of post-1917 Russia and to explain its failures either by the legacy of tsarism or by foreign hostility, or, if all else failed, by the inherent difficulties of trying to construct a totally new kind of society based on social equality and justice. I find that German historians are particularly averse to criticizing the communist past and grow positively livid at any suggestion of parallels between National Socialism and communism. Their impassioned refusal even to consider such links, their harassment of anyone who calls attention to them, suggests that they have a psychic need to disassociate themselves from Nazism: for, since the Nazis were anti-Communist, anti-communism is, for them, tainted with Nazism. English-language scholars, who have no guilt feelings about Nazism, unless they are sympathetic to Communism, experience fewer difficulties treating this issue on its merits.

Whatever the reasons, during the past three decades there has occurred a convergence of approaches between Soviet and Western historiography of the revolution and its immediate aftermath. The prevailing view among Western historians is that the fall of tsarism as well as the triumph of Bolshevism were preordained, whereas the emergence of Stalin as Lenin's successor was something of a mishap. Just exactly why this mishap occurred, they have been unable, up to now, to explain.

The central issue on which the revisionist school challenged the orthodox version concerned the events of October 1917. The question was whether Bolshevik power seizure was a genuine revolution or an ordinary *coup d'état*: whether the Bolsheviks rode to power on a wave of popular support or whether, like thieves in the night, they stole it. Western historians — particularly those of the younger generation — have increasingly adopted the Soviet point of view, that October 1917 was indeed a popular revolution in which the Bolsheviks acted in response to pressure from the masses. My thesis is precisely the opposite to that advanced by the revisionists, which, by now, is virtually obligatory in Western universities. I shall argue that there was nothing preordained about either the fall of tsarism or the Bolshevik power seizure. In fact, I feel that the latter was something of a fluke, but that, once it occurred and the totalitarian machine was in place, then the rise of Stalin became virtually a foregone conclusion.

Causes, which are what the question "Why?" is meant to address, are the most difficult aspect of the historian's craft because they function on so many different levels. I have used the following analogy before, but because it is apt I will recall it to illustrate what I mean. When you shake an apple tree and apples come cascading down, what "causes" them to fall? Is it the shaking of the tree? Is it the ripeness of the fruit which would have made them fall down, sooner or later, anyway? Or is it the law of gravity which makes objects fall downward to earth? In dealing with human events, we find similar levels of explanation, from the most specific to the most general, and it is next to impossible to ascertain which of them determines the outcome. Usually, as in the case of the apple tree, one finds causes operating in tandem on three distinct levels: the *longue durée*, the intermediate span, and the short term — in the last of which accidents play a prominent role.

The *longue durée* refers to trends over which neither individuals nor groups exert control; they are processes rather than events, and move glacially on their own. The decline of Rome, to cite one example, was an occurrence that no one could have prevented: decay was built into the system, and the rot progressed slowly until the system collapsed. Then, there are medium-term developments where individuals acting alone or in groups do make a difference: let me cite as an illustration the American

Revolution and the constitutional arrangement that issued from it. And, finally, there are accidents. On the eve of the Bolshevik coup on the night of October 24, 1917, Lenin emerged from one of the hideaways in which he had taken refuge since early July to escape the police, who had orders for his arrest. He made his way to Smolnyi, the headquarters of the Bolshevik command, with his face bandaged, looking as if he were on his way to the dentist. He was stopped by a mounted patrol. When asked for his identity papers, Lenin pretended to be drunk, so they let him go. Had he been arrested, the Bolshevik coup might very well have never occurred, because he was the principal driving force behind it and the only person with a plan of action. Similarly, if Fannie Kaplan — the Socialist Revolutionary terrorist who shot Lenin in August 1918 — had not suffered from defective eyesight and had aimed her gun just one millimetre more to the right or the left, he would have been dead, and the Bolshevik regime, already in deep trouble, would very likely have fallen apart.

My scholarly experience of nearly half a century, reinforced by a two-year stint in Washington, persuades me that it is entirely futile to seek any single explanation for major occurrences. Like a surgeon, the historian has to make skilful use of all kinds of instruments if he wishes to uncover the causes of non-specific events. Any one explanation is bound to be wrong.

Psychologically, it is natural to assume that whatever has happened had to happen. This perception is often translated by those addicted to it into scientific terms, but in fact it rests on a very primitive psychology. It is hard for most people to imagine that events did not have to happen the way they did because doing so forces them to confront the question: "If it could have happened otherwise, why didn't it?" This fatalistic attitude holds true of revisionist historians' treatment of the collapse of tsarism. Historians of the left have been busy arguing that its fall was inevitable whether or not Russia had been involved in the First World War, but this assertion is apparent only in hindsight. It would be good if such historians could predict the future as accurately as they predict the past: for it so happens that not one of the proponents of historical inevitability where the fall of tsarism is concerned had been able to foresee the dissolution of the Soviet Union. If you read the Russian and foreign press before 1917, or memoirs of the time, you find that hardly anyone expected the downfall of tsarism either. On the contrary, people believed that tsarism would survive for a long time to come. One of the reasons the Russian radical revolutionaries, and even liberals, acted with such reckless abandon against the regime was their conviction that they could do so with impunity because it was virtually indestructible. For had not tsarism weathered all onslaughts and all crises, and emerged from them intact? This was especially true of the Revolution of 1905, which at its climax looked as if it would bring the regime down. And yet, within two years of having made some political concessions in the

October Manifesto, the regime restored order and was firmly back in the saddle. Suffice it to say that as late as January 1917, when he was an exile in Switzerland, Lenin predicted that he and his generation would not live to see a revolution in Russia. This he said seven weeks before tsarism collapsed. If there was anyone in Europe who understood the weaknesses of tsarist Russia it was Lenin, and yet even he did not foresee its imminent demise, so obvious to revisionist historians viewing the event *ex post facto*.

Another item of evidence indicating that contemporaries believed in tsarism's durability is that foreigners, mainly the French but not only they, invested heavily in late tsarist Russia. Billions of dollars were spent on Russian obligations and securities, nearly all of which would be lost in 1918, with the Bolshevik repudiation of state debts and nationalization of private enterprises.

Some historians who argue the inevitability of the collapse of tsarism point for proof to the extraordinary number of industrial strikes that occurred in Russia on the eve of the First World War. This argument, however, cannot withstand scrutiny. While, indeed, there was an unprecedented number of strikes in Russia at that time, exactly the same phenomenon occurred in England and the United States. Both of these countries experienced a surge of industrial stoppages on the eve of August 1914, and yet neither had a revolution. Industrial action is rarely political in motivation and, therefore, hardly a reliable symptom of a regime's imminent collapse. In Russia, strikes were, first and foremost, a manifestation of the growing strength of organized labour. Until 1905, tsarism had outlawed trade unions and ruthlessly suppressed strikes. After 1905–6, trade unions were legalized and so were strikes. Hence, stoppages occurred with increasing frequency as organized labour struggled for better working conditions and wages.

The single most important factor making for stability — at any rate, for the time being — was that the Russian village remained quiet. Three-quarters of the Empire's population made a living from agriculture. Pre–1914 Russia had approximately one hundred million peasants and only between two and three million workers, of whom one-third or so were peasants employed seasonally in railway construction and maintenance, and therefore hardly "workers" in the customary sense. From the point of view of the tsarist police, even if there was endemic unrest among workers, as long as the village remained tranquil — and it did so immediately before and during the war, owing to bountiful harvests and high prices commanded by agricultural produce — the situation was under control.

I have showed why tsarism need not have collapsed. Now the question arises, why did it collapse? In order to respond we must rid ourselves of the Marxist notion that all historical events are determined by social conflicts — as the Communist Manifesto puts it, that all history is the history of class war. This thesis is simply not sustainable. Indeed, history knows many instances of class conflict, but it also knows events that have very different causes: political, ideological, religious, and so on. As I have said before, any unilinear explanation of historical phenomena like the Marxist one is bound to be false, and can be sustained only by ignoring events that do not fit the class interpretation or by stretching them on the Procrustean bed of economic determinism until they do. Let me remind you of the revolution that occurred in Russia as recently as August 1991. The collapse of the Soviet Union, a state which appeared as solidly entrenched to us as the tsarist Empire did in its day, was not triggered by social unrest: there were no strike waves, no massive demonstrations, no widespread violence. The USSR disintegrated because of political decisions made at the top. I am not surprised that the revisionist historians who see the cause of the collapse of tsarism in alleged social unrest do not apply the same methodology to the collapse of the Soviet Union: if they were to do so, they would confront a void. And this would subvert their whole picture of 1917.

In both cases — the collapse of tsarism in March 1917 and the collapse of the Soviet Union in August 1991 — the world was caught unawares. With one exception, I do not know of a single Westerner who foresaw the latter. The solitary exception was the English journalist Bernard Levin, who in 1979 predicted that in ten years the Berlin Wall would come down. He is proud of this prediction, and justifiably so. But he did not provide any explanation for why this was bound to happen, or, in retrospect, why it did happen, so I suspect his was just a fortunate guess.

I am highly sceptical of the whole socialist-Marxist approach to history, particularly revolutionary history, because I find that when the so-called masses are discontented, they are inspired by specific grievances that are capable of being satisfied within the existing system. Only intellectuals have universal grievances: only they believe that nothing can change unless everything changes. This is not true of the people at large, whether peasants or workers. In the spring of 1905, the Russian monarchy invited the population to submit complaints to the government. Hundreds of such *cahiers* were sent in. According to recent analyses, none called for a fundamental change of the regime, that is, abolition of the monarchy. The peasants demanded lower taxes and more land; the workers wanted an eight-hour working day and the right to unionize; the minorities clamoured for greater autonomy. All these demands could well have been accommodated within the existing regime had the rulers found the courage to do so, and the intelligentsia the good sense to assist it.

Students of revolutions have observed that, as a rule, the grievances of the people look backward rather than forward. Rather than clamour for new rights, people complain of being unjustly deprived of ancient rights, real or imagined. That held true of Russia, particularly as regards land, the single most explosive social issue. The peasants firmly believed that God had created land, just as he had created air and water, for everyone's enjoyment and benefit. One could use it, but not own it. They wanted the abolition of private property in land, not as a revolutionary act paving the way to socialism (as many revolutionaries wrongly misunderstood them), but as a return to tradition, to an order they believed had existed since time immemorial. One student of Russia wrote that the *muzhik* (the peasant) could no more conceive of a change of regimes than of a change of climate: to him, the tsar and everything that went with him were a given.

It was the radical intellectuals who deliberately channelled the specific dissatisfactions of the population at large into a wholesale rejection of the political and social system. This was the tactic employed by the liberal-dominated Union of Unions in 1905, when it developed the strategy of having every one of the many professional and trade organizations affiliated with it politicize its demands. For example, when a trade union would call for shorter working hours or higher wages, the intellectuals in the Union of Unions would assure it that such limited objectives could not be attained unless the country's entire political system were demolished, and the absolute monarchy replaced with a parliamentary democracy and a constitution. The workers could not care less about parliament and a constitution, but this demand was inserted into their petitions by liberal intellectuals. This is what occurred in the famous procession on so-called Bloody Sunday, January 9, 1905, which ended in the massacre that unleashed the First Russian Revolution.

Before proceeding to the intelligentsia, let me discuss the endemic weaknesses of the tsarist state that made it vulnerable to the kind of assaults to which it was subjected in the early years of the century and which contributed greatly to its ultimate demise. When one studies Russian history from the vantage point of European history, one becomes aware that, from its foundation, the Russian state was imposed from above rather than emerging from below. The population was a mere object of state authority. In this respect, Russia was very Oriental. The Empire was traditionally run by a bureaucracy and a gentry, after 1880 reinforced by a political-police organization. This political policing was a Russian invention; Russia was the first country to have two police systems, one to protect the state from its citizens, and the other to protect the citizens from each other. Subsequently, this dual structure became a fundamental feature of totalitarian states.

Studying Russian history from the West European perspective, one also becomes conscious of the effect that the absence of feudalism had on Russia. Feudalism had created in the West networks of economic and political institutions that served the central state, once it replaced the feudal system, as a source of social support and relative stability. Russia knew no feudalism in the traditional sense of the word, since, after the emergence of the Muscovite monarchy in the fifteenth and sixteenth centuries, all landowners were tenants-in-chief of the Crown, and subinfeudation was unknown. As a result, all power was concentrated in the Crown. The lines of authority ran from the top down; there were hardly any lateral lines. The fact that the wires were concentrated in the hands of the Crown and its staff meant that in a time of crisis the state would instantly disintegrate: for once the monarch went, these wires snapped and there was nothing left to hold the country together.

This is what happened in 1917, and again in 1991. When the reins controlled exclusively by the Politburo and the Central Committee were broken during disagreements within the party's directing organs, Russia fell apart, and did so as instantly as tsarism had seventy-four years earlier.

It is striking how quickly Germany got back on her feet politically after the débâcle of 1918. The Kaiser fled to Holland, soviets were sprouting everywhere, yet, within three or four months, a National Assembly was elected and a democratic government took office. In Russia this did not occur; for while, in Germany society, the force "below" stepped in to fill the temporary vacuum; in Russia, when there was nothing at the top, there was nothing below either. Only another authoritarian regime, imposed from above, could restore a semblance of order.

So, around 1900, we have a mechanically rather than organically structured state that denies the population any voice in government, and yet, at the same time, aspires to the status of a world power. This aspiration compels it to promote industrial development and higher education, which has the inevitable effect of shifting much opinion and the power to make decisions to private citizens. Pre–1905 tsarism thus suffered from an irreconcilable contradiction. A not-insignificant segment of the population received secondary and higher education, acquiring, in the process, Western attitudes, and yet it was treated as being on the same level with the illiterate peasantry, that is, as unfit to participate in the affairs of state. Capitalist industrialists and bankers made major decisions affecting the country's economy and employment, and yet had no say in that country's politics because politics was the monopoly of the bureaucracy. I may remind you that, in Imperial Russia (as, *mutatis mutandis*, in Soviet Russia), one had to have official rank, or *chin*, in order to qualify for a governmental position. This practice precluded the kind of participation of civilians in administration which is common in Western democracies, leaving the entire sphere of politics in the hands of professional officials. And these officials swore an oath of loyalty to the person of the tsar, not to the nation at large or the state, and regarded themselves as royal stewards rather than public servants.

The result was a situation which Marx had rightly predicted had to arise when the political form — in this case, heavily centralized and static — no longer corresponded to the socio-economic content — increasingly dispersed and dynamic. Such a situation is by its very nature fraught with explosive potential. In 1982, when I worked in the National Security Council, I was asked to contribute ideas to a major speech that President Reagan was scheduled to deliver in London. My contribution consisted of a reference to Marx's dictum that, when there develops a significant disparity between the political form and the socio-economic content, the prospect is revolution. This disparity, however, had now developed in the Soviet Union, not in the capitalist West. President Reagan inserted this thought into his speech, and the reaction in Moscow was one of uncontrolled fury: this, of course, was language they well understood and interpreted to mean a declaration of political warfare against the Communist Bloc. Their anger was enhanced by the awareness that the statement was correct, that they were ruling in a manner that did not correspond to either the economic or the cultural level of their population.

Much the same held true of pre-revolutionary Russia. In October 1905, following defeats in the war with Japan and nationwide disorders which accompanied them, the tsarist government found itself compelled to grant the country a constitution and a parliament. This was certainly a step in the right direction, narrowing the immense gap that had developed between the political form and the socio-economic as well as cultural content. But, for various reasons, the reforms granted in 1905 and 1906 were soon emasculated. The Crown, supported by reactionary groups, did not honour the concessions it had made, because they had been wrested from it at gunpoint, while the liberal and radical intelligentsia, treating these concessions as a prelude to true democracy, refused to operate within their limits. Thus, each protagonist, in his own way, sabotaged the 1905–6 constitutional arrangement, and the old tensions remained. This is not to say that Russia was seething with revolutionary ardour. I find no evidence for that. What I do find is specific grievances such as exist to a greater or smaller degree in any society, but in Russia's case found inadequate outlets for resolution. In genuine democracies, when these grievances accumulate they are satisfied by quiet revolutions called "elections." In the November 1994 congressional elections in the United States, the voters gave an unmistakable signal of dissatisfaction with existing conditions by defeating every candidate of the ruling Democratic Party. The result has been a sea-change in the make-up of Congress and a startlingly quick shift in the behaviour of the Democratic White House. But in tsarist Russia such possibilities did not exist. Disaffection accumulated and, by the winter of 1916–17, the mood of the urban population, provoked by inflation and shortages, turned decidedly ugly.

Finally, I want to call your attention to the peasant problem, which hung over Russia like a black cloud following the emancipation of the serfs in 1861 and which the Soviet government "solved" in its own way by abolishing communal landholding and killing off millions of peasants. I refer to the previously mentioned refusal of the Russian *muzhik* to acknowledge the fact of private landownership. This is a pre-modern attitude, shared by many primitive peoples. In the case of Russia, it had its roots in a kind of collective memory of a Golden Age, when land was available for the asking because the country had a tiny population scattered over a boundless territory. As late as the turn of the twentieth century, most Russians, educated and uneducated alike, believed that, if private landholding were abolished, there would be plenty for all who wished to cultivate. In fact, there was not enough. The population was growing at an extraordinarily rapid rate, with an annual excess of between fifteen and eighteen live births over deaths per thousand inhabitants. Prime Minister Peter Stolypin calculated how many hectares of land were needed each year just to feed this new population and concluded they were not to be procured by any means, even wholesale confiscation. The only solution to rural overpopulation was an increase in yields per hectare and industrialization. But the money required significantly to improve yields was not available, and industry, while expanding, did not grow rapidly enough to employ much of the excess rural labour. The consequence was an explosive situation which various programs initiated by Stolypin, such as resettlement and transfer of state properties to peasants, might have mitigated had there been enough time and had the radical intellectuals not incited the peasants to take the law into their own hands.

In sum, you had in late Imperial Russia serious tensions caused partly by the unwillingness of tsarism to democratize, and partly by the long-term, potentially explosive mood of the Russian village, which could not find enough land to employ all those living in it. But the really critical factor, the factor that transformed specific complaints into an all-encompassing rejection of the existing political, economic, and social order, was the intelligentsia. The Russian intelligentsia, both radical and liberal, stood far to the left of its West European counterpart, filled with utopian ideals which it had absorbed from Western literary sources but had no opportunity to try out in practice. People who come into power with plans of grand reforms as a rule quickly realize, if able to test those plans, that ingrained habits and vested interests set limits to what they can accomplish. The Clinton Administration, for example, which took office with rather radical ideas born in the heady atmosphere of the 1960s, learned in no time that ideas which look good on paper can be next to impossible to implement, no matter how noble the intention. But if ambitious would-be reformers lack the opportunity to learn from experience, they not only adhere to their utopian ideals but become ever more fanatically committed to them, certain that, with sufficient determination and force, they should be able to make them work.

Russian radicals, in some measure backed by liberals, opposed reforms because they threatened to prevent revolution, their ultimate objective. In 1906–7, several attempts were made to bring liberals into the cabinet: each time, they refused out of fear of being compromised. The radical intelligentsia incessantly appealed to the population to ostracize the government and have nothing to do with it. When the government did nothing, the intelligentsia accused it of passivity; when it made concessions, the intelligentsia felt they had the bureaucrats on the run.

Thus, when the liberals won the elections to the first Duma in 1906, they immediately decided that the new constitution was entirely inadequate, and that what the country needed was a Constituent Assembly which would proclaim a Russian republic. This attitude led to incessant conflicts in Russia's first representative legislative body. There was simply no possibility for any kind of compromise to be forged. Later on, during the war, the tsarist government attempted to make peace with the opposition by granting the Duma in fact, if not in name, much of what it wanted, such as the power informally to approve of ministerial appointments. It invariably met with rebuffs. The intelligentsia treated every conciliatory move by the government as another sign of weakness and an opportunity to press for more demands.

So much for the long-term and intermediate factors accounting for the collapse of tsarism. Let me now turn to short-term ones. These factors had much to do with the First World War. As we know, the war imposed tremendous strains on all belligerent countries. While it had been widely expected that the coming world conflict would be decided in three, or, at most, six months, it lasted for over four years. And the countries that survived its unprecedented tensions were those able to create governments of national unity in which state authority and politicians of all persuasions buried their differences and joined forces to work for victory. Such cooperation was simply not possible in Russia: there, mutual suspicions ran too deep. The government feared that any concessions it made during wartime to politicians from among the intelligentsia — for example, by yielding to the Duma the right formally to appoint ministers — would, after the war, enable the intellectuals to take over the government and reduce the Crown to ceremonial functions. The intellectuals, for their part, saw any victory of the government, whether military or political, as strengthening the monarchy and its officialdom, and thus setting back the prospects of democracy and socialism. The sense of national unity was too weakly developed in Russia for appeals to patriotism to have much effect, except momentarily and mainly in the form of xenophobia.

I know of no belligerent country in Europe during the First World War where there was as much tension between government and educated society as in Russia, where the two forces that held the destiny of the nation in their hands, instead of cooperating, engaged in incessant feuding. And such animosity in time of war, especially a war of attrition, was, of course, fatal. There were people in the Russian government who maintained that the real enemy was not the Germans or the Austrians, but domestic liberals and radicals. And there were socialists and liberals — among them, Duma deputy Alexander Kerensky — who claimed that the real enemy was not the Germans or the Austrians, but tsarist bureaucrats. When one reads the irresponsible speeches delivered in the Duma under the protection of parliamentary immunity during 1915 and 1916, in the very heat of war, one can only marvel that Russia stayed intact as long as she did. It seems to me that the unrelenting hostility between the government and the political opposition was the prime immediate cause of the regime's collapse. The government, driven against the wall, made concession after concession, and yet nothing was enough because the liberals and radicals were sharpening weapons for the *coup de grâce.*

Another related factor was the widespread belief in treason in high places. The Russian army had suffered a humiliating defeat at the hands of the Germans in 1915 when it had to abandon Poland, recently conquered Galicia, and much of the land along the Baltic coast — all exceptionally rich and populous areas. Russians found it difficult to accept that they had been bested in a fair fight by a superior force; the loss had to be due to treason. And, as misfortune would want it, the wife of the tsar was a German — a very patriotic lady, devoted to Russia, but nevertheless widely believed to be a spy who betrayed to her native land the military secrets of her acquired homeland and conspired to sign a separate peace. The suspicions of treason in high places received reinforcement from the appointment, in late 1916, as prime minister a Russian with a German name, Boris Stürmer. We have at our disposal police reports from that time which summarize letters sent home by front-line soldiers, as well as letters sent to them by their families, which are filled with such rumours. None of the charges levelled at the tsarina or the prime minister had any substance; in fact, they were a tissue of lies concocted by politicians willing to use any tool to embarrass the government. The animosity towards the Crown brought into being an unprecedented alliance of radicals and liberals, who hated it on principle, with conservative nationalists, who acted out of dismay over the alleged betrayal of Russia to the German enemy. This coalition left the government friendless and defenceless.

It is a mistake to attribute the February Revolution to fatigue with the war. The contrary is true. Russians wanted to pursue the war more effectively, and they felt that the existing government was not capable of doing it, that existing political structures were in need of a major overhaul: remove the disloyal tsarina and let the Duma appoint ministers, whereupon Russia will really be able to fight properly and win. Fatigue with the war set in only after the unsuccessful June 1917 offensive launched by the Provisional Government to bolster its prestige and lift national morale. Until then, even the Bolsheviks did not dare openly to call for peace because it was a highly unpopular slogan.

The tsar, of course, could have saved the throne if that were his supreme objective. All he had to do was to sign a separate peace, exactly as Lenin would do in March 1918. If he had concluded such a peace with the Germans and the Austrians — and he would have found them most receptive because both powers were eager to end the fighting on the Eastern Front in order to concentrate all their forces in the West — the First World War might have ended quite differently. Had he done so, say, in late 1916, bringing home millions of combat troops capable of quelling domestic disorder, the Germans might well have crushed the Allies in France and Belgium, and the Russian Revolution would have been averted. But being a devoted Russian patriot and loyal ally, he would not even contemplate such action. And when he was told by the generals that the hostility towards him and his wife had reached such a pitch of intensity that, for Russia to stay in the war, he had to abdicate, he abdicated. He took this step out of pure patriotism. Having studied in minute detail the massive information regarding the steps leading up to the abdication of Nicholas II, I have not the slightest doubt that he faced no popular pressures to abdicate; the pressure stemmed exclusively from the ranks of politicians and generals who thought the Crown's removal essential to victory. The fact that the tsar's abdication had the opposite effect of that intended tells nothing of his motives in so doing.

I have no illusion that I have cited all the factors responsible for the collapse of tsarism. There were others, some of which I will enumerate quickly. One worthy of mention is the loss of prestige of the tsarist government due to a series of military and diplomatic humiliations which Russia had suffered since the Crimean War.

In the eighteenth and the first half of the nineteenth century, Russia marched from victory to victory; then, unexpectedly, with the outbreak of the Crimean War, she suffered defeat after defeat. This very negatively affected popular attitudes towards the regime. Because it maintained itself essentially by force, if tsarism was unable to defeat foreign powers, then there surely was something wrong with it. The débâcle in Poland in 1915, to which I had alluded, was for many Russians the last straw. It proved to them conclusively that tsarism, or, at any rate, the reigning tsar, was incompetent to carry out its supreme mission, which was to expand Russia's territory and defend it from foreign enemies. And who knows? Perhaps we will learn one day, when all the archives have been thrown open, that the Soviet Army's reverses in Afghanistan played a similar role in the downfall of communism.

The breakdown of transport during the First World War contributed to the unhappiness of the urban population because it seriously hampered the delivery of food and fuel to the northern cities, where the food riots started. Inflation in the cities also played its part.

I hope I have conveyed the image of a power that, however dazzling its external glitter, was internally weak and quite unable to cope effectively with the strains — political, economic, and psychological — which the war brought in its wake. In my opinion, the principal causes of the downfall in 1917 (as also in 1991) were political, and not economic or social. The difference between then and now is that, in 1917, you had intellectuals gathered in political parties that had well-formulated programs for drastic change, whereas today there are only politicians interested in power, but without any clear motive about where to take the country.

CHAPTER TWO:

Why Did the Bolsheviks Triumph?

THE SECOND ENIGMA of the Russian Revolution is why the Bolsheviks won. During and immediately after the October 1917 revolution, the event was generally perceived as a classic *coup d'état* rather than a popular revolution, and the Bolsheviks' victory was attributed not to their popular support but to their superior organization and greater ruthlessness. This interpretation, formulated by participants and eyewitnesses, dominated Western historical scholarship for half a century.

Interestingly enough, it received tacit support from both Lenin and Trotsky, neither of whom ever claimed — as far as I am able to determine from their voluminous writings — that the Bolsheviks emerged victorious because they had the masses behind them. Trotsky wrote in his *History of the Russian Revolution* [L. Trotskii, *Istoriia Russkoi Revoliutsii*, Vol. II, pt. 2 (Berlin, 1933), 319] that 25,000 or 30,000 people, at most, took part in the events of October in Petrograd; this, in a city of 2 million, and in a country of some 150 million. Lenin, himself, had unconcealed contempt for the masses and their ability to do anything beyond surviving. I do not know whether he had read Vilfredo Pareto or Gaetano Mosca, but he certainly shared their faith in political élites. The following is a quotation from one of Lenin's writings dating from July 1917:

> In times of revolution it is not enough to ascertain the "will of the majority." No — one must *be stronger* at the decisive moment, in the decisive place, and *win*. Beginning with the medieval "peasant war" in Germany... until 1905, we see countless instances of how the better organized, more conscious, better-armed minority imposed its will on the majority and conquered it.

These are remarkable words from a self-styled Marxist revolutionary. But the argument makes sense, given that the Bolsheviks' constituency at the time was quite small, even among workers. We know that, in late 1917, only slightly more than 5 per cent of Russia's industrial workers belonged to the Communist Party, in a country in which industrial workers represented only 1 or 1.5 per cent of the population.

It was thus the unspoken perception of the Bolshevik leaders, and the explicit one of the earlier generation of historians, that October 1917 was a *perevorot* — an "overthrow" — rather than a *revoliutsiia* — an action accomplished by a "better organized, more conscious, better-armed minority [which] imposed its will on the majority and conquered it." In other words, a *coup d'é-tat*. In the 1930s, eager to acquire credit for his alleged role in the October events, Stalin began to talk increasingly of the role of the party in winning the October Revolution, a view he imposed on the Soviet historical profession. But after his death, because Stalin had become unsavoury and the party wanted to disassociate itself from him, the emphasis was shifted increasingly to the population at large. By the 1960s, Communist historians began to stress the alleged role of the "popular masses" (the German *Volksmassen*) in the Bolshevik triumph.

This theme was picked up by the younger generation of Western historians in the 1960s — the era of *détente* — who, for various reasons to which I have alluded, including disgust with America's role in Vietnam and its allegedly provocative pursuit of the Cold War, fell in step with the Soviet historical profession. They, too, came to stress the popular involvement in the events of October and to argue that, far from imposing their will on the people, the Bolsheviks had been forced into action by them. Except for a less adulatory tone in regard to the classics of Marxism–Leninism and a certain respect for Western scholarly manners (not always, however, observed), the works of these "revisionists" hardly differed in substance from those of their Soviet counterparts.

Let me turn next to the origins and character of the Bolshevik Party. Despite its name — derived from the Russian adjective *bol'she*, signifying "more" or "greater" — before 1917 the Bolsheviks were the smallest of the three main Russian radical parties: most of the time they had fewer followers than their Social-Democratic rivals, the Mensheviks, and many fewer than the Socialists-Revolutionaries. The composition of their membership was heavily Great Russian. Statistics of the Fifth Congress of the Social Democratic Party, which met in 1907 when the Bolsheviks and Mensheviks were still partners, indicate that 78.3 per cent of the Bolshevik candidates came from the Great Russian provinces. Among the Mensheviks, the proportion of Great Russians was less than half that number (34 per cent), the majority consisting of Georgians, Jews, and other ethnic minorities. The party preserved the Great Russian make-up throughout its history. Thus, in the elections to the Constituent Assembly held in November 1917, the bulk of the Bolshevik vote came from the Great Russian provinces. And during the Civil War, it was the Great Russian centre that provided the Soviet regime with the bulk of manpower. Referring to these facts, the Russian émigré historian N.N. Golovin observed that the strongest support for the Bolsheviks came from the regions which before 1861 had had the highest incidence of serfdom.

The theoretical basis of the Bolshevik Party was Lenin's belief — also quite un-Marxist — that the working class in and of itself is not revolutionary. He reached this conclusion on the basis of his own experiences with labour in St. Petersburg during the mid-1890s, the only period in his life when he had direct contact with the so-called proletariat. In observing the behaviour of Russian as well as West European workers, he concluded that, left to their own devices, workers were incapable of progressing beyond trade unionism, that is, organizations dedicated to extracting the maximal economic concessions from the capitalist class while leaving the capitalist system intact.

From this evidence it was possible to draw two practical inferences. One, that revolution was an unrealistic objective and that the socialists should concentrate on helping labour secure better economic conditions, expecting to gain power some time in the future through the ballot box rather than the barricade. This was the trend which came to prevail in the European socialist movement in the late nineteenth century following the emergence of Bernsteinianism, a reformist movement within German Social-Democracy. But, for Lenin, for whom the revolution was an end in itself, this was no answer. He concluded that, if the workers were not revolutionary, then the revolution had to be brought to them from the outside. This necessarily implied that the bearers of the revolution would not be rank-and-file workers, since they were poisoned by the bacillus of accommodation, but by full-time, professional revolutionaries. Here are Lenin's observations on the subject, which to the modern ear have a remarkably "fascist" ring:

> No single class in history has ever attained mastery unless it has produced political leaders... capable of organizing the movement and leading it.... It is necessary to prepare men who devote to the revolution, not only their free evenings, but their entire lives.

This tenet had a variety of ramifications. But it meant, above all, that the people who led the revolution could not be workers because workers could not devote their "entire lives" to political work: after all, they had to earn a living. So, even if they happened to be workers originally, once they joined the movement they were required to turn into party *apparatchiks*.

In 1900, after suffering a severe psychological crisis brought on by the spread of Bernstein's ideas to the Russian Social-Democratic movement, Lenin declared that "the labour movement separated from Social Democracy... inevitably turns bourgeois." This sentiment subverted the very essence of Marxism, to which Lenin pledged undeviating loyalty. According to Marx, the evolution of capitalism would inevitably lead to the pauperization of the proletariat and then, just as inevitably, to its radicalization.

It is interesting that Benito Mussolini arrived at an identical judgment ten years later. Before the outbreak of the First World War, Mussolini had been the closest analogue to Lenin in the European socialist movement, being equally revolutionary and anti-reformist. He was the Lenin of the Italian Socialist Party with the difference that, whereas Mussolini managed to rally behind him a revolutionary majority and expel the reformers, in Russia, Lenin found himself leading a minority and forced to break away from the Social-Democratic Establishment. Unfortunately, it is not possible to ascertain whether Mussolini arrived at this position independently or under the influence of Lenin. We cannot determine whether or not he had met Lenin during their common exile in Switzerland; Mussolini once cryptically remarked: "Lenin knew me better than I knew him." I suspect that the ideas of political élitism, *Führertum*, as well as ethnic and social extermination, were so much in the air in pre–First World War Europe that it is not necessary to seek for them specific sources.

In the early years of the twentieth century, Lenin resolved that he had to form a novel political party which would inculcate revolutionary socialism in the working class and, concurrently, prepare itself for the seizure of power at the opportune moment. This moment was linked in his mind with a general European war. In a postcard to his mistress, Inessa Armand, sent in July 1914, days or possibly even hours before war had been declared, he wrote in his awkward English: "Best greetings for the commencing revolution in Russia." Apparently he concluded from the experience of the Russo–Japanese War that the carnage would radicalize the masses, especially in his own country, and make revolution all but inevitable. (Incidentally, the future Italian Fascists entertained similar hopes: Mussolini, like Lenin, believed that, left to themselves, workers were pacifistic and eager to compromise, for which reason he attached great importance to war as a catalyst of revolution.)

There is a peculiar anti-democratic, reactionary element in Bolshevism which prompted some to deny that it was socialist, even if it was not clear precisely what it was. The concept of totalitarianism had not yet been invented, and no one could anticipate that Lenin's party was a precursor of a new type of political organization that would be emulated before long by mass-based dictators of both the internationalist ("left-wing") and nationalist ("right-wing") varieties. The party which Lenin forged and led was really not a party, in the customary sense of the word. It was more of an "order," in the sense in which Hitler called his National–Socialist Party "ein Orden," bound by the members' unshakable loyalty to their leader and one another, but subject to no other principle and responsible to no other constituency. Genuine political parties strive to enlarge their membership, whereas these pseudo-parties — the Bolshevik one first, and the Fascist and the Nazi ones later — were exclusive in that they treated membership as a privilege, restricting it to persons who met certain ideological as well as class or racial criteria. Elements regarded as unworthy were purged.

The purpose of totalitarian parties, for which Bolshevism provided the model, was not to become the government but to manipulate the government from behind the scenes. The brotherhood of the elect was designed to stand outside the body politic even as they directed its every move. Once in power, the new rulers created a "dual state" under which ordinary government institutions, with their ministries and judiciary, served as a façade, concealing the real authority, which was in the hands of the party. Mussolini aptly called his Fascist Party "the capillary organization" of the political body. The prototype in this respect, too, was Lenin's Bolshevik organization. Typically, totalitarian parties did not compete with rival parties, but liquidated them.

In July 1992, I happened to be in Moscow, working in archives which had just been made available to foreigners, when the trial of the Communist Party got under way. I was requested by the Russian Constitutional Court to give an opinion on whether the CPSU was a political party or not: the question was asked in connection with the charge that had led to its outlawing by President Yeltsin the previous year. In response I said that, indeed, the CPSU neither was nor had ever been a party in any accepted sense, but rather, as the prosecution claimed, a special "mechanism" for seizing control of the state. The court sustained the president's decree, even as it hedged on drawing from it the appropriate conclusions.

The Bolshevik Party was small in early 1917, partly because of defections during the relatively calm and prosperous Stolypin period, partly because of the rather savage persecution by the police after the outbreak of the First World War, which it opposed. The police had thoroughly penetrated the party with its agents. Suffice it to say that the chief spokesman for the Bolshevik Party in the Duma worked for the Okhrana, the Imperial security police. So did the editor of *Pravda*, Lenin's principal organ: all of Lenin's articles in *Pravda* published before July 1914, when it was closed, were vetted by the police.

Notwithstanding their minuscule membership and the police penetration, the Bolsheviks enjoyed some important advantages over their rivals.

Lenin treated politics as warfare. Of course, all Marxists did so in a sense; to the Marxist, politics means class war. But the others did not take this dictum quite as literally as did Lenin. Whereas they thought of it as ordinary conflict, he and he alone saw its purpose as conquering power and annihilating all rivals. By annihilation, he meant, not merely eliminating them as competitors, but physically exterminating them. Such a view of politics, of course, gave Lenin great advantages in the struggle for power. Once power was gained, however, and the adversary was "conquered," such a view provided no guidance for running a society.

The Bolsheviks felt no qualms in resorting to "merciless" terror (the adjective was often used by Lenin, for he thought Russians "too soft" to act with the requisite ruthlessness). The Communist historical establishment and those among Western scholars who shared its general outlook have maintained that early Bolshevik terror had been a regrettable but unavoidable response to the "counter-revolutionary" activities of the regime's opponents. This argument was never persuasive, given that the Cheka, or secret police, the main agency of the "Red Terror," was established in December 1917, before there was any organized resistance to the new regime. Now we find confirmation of these doubts in a document released by what was previously called the Central Party Archive. Handwritten by Lenin, it calls for the "urgent" unleashing of terror and requests that a meeting be held (among the participants, he mentions Felix Dzerzhinskii, the future head of the political police) in order to discuss its realization. The document is undated, and the Russian archivists, for reasons best known to them, assign it to 1920. Internal evidence as well as the letterhead on which the note was written, however, leave no doubt that it originated sometime in the summer or early fall of 1918. It confirms that the "Red Terror" was not a reluctant response to the actions of others but a prophylactic measure designed to nip in the bud any thought of resistance to the dictatorship. Both Lenin and Dzerzhinskii later claimed that the Cheka and its terror had saved "the revolution." This is correct, but only if by "revolution" one means Lenin's party.

Lenin saw himself as the commander-in-chief of a organization committed to permanent political warfare. He unquestionably excelled in this particular pursuit. In the concluding chapter of *Russia under the Bolshevik Regime*, I maintain that he was never an outstanding statesman — he had few constructive ideas — but that he was one of the great conquerors of world history, a man who vanquished his own country in a way that no one before him had even attempted. The rival parties, the socialists and, to some extent, the liberals, were populist, believing in the innate wisdom of the Russian people. They were not prepared to fight, and they lost out to a politician for whom struggle was a normal occupation, and peace a mere breathing-spell for war.

Lenin wanted power. This may sound self-evident: after all, every politican is assumed to lust for power. But deep down, Lenin's rivals did not want it. I see parallels in today's Russia: Yeltsin wants to rule; most of his rivals fear the responsibility of power, preferring to criticize from the sidelines. In 1917, the Socialists-Revolutionaries and the Mensheviks were quite content to let the "bourgeois" Provisional Government govern while they kept up a steady barrage of denunciation and criticism. But Lenin wanted much more. There is a famous incident in April 1917 which came to figure prominently in Soviet hagiography. Lenin had just returned to Russia from Switzerland.

His followers lined up with the Mensheviks in expressing satisfaction with an arrangement under which the socialists, through the soviets, controlled the "bourgeoisie" and prevented it from straying from the democratic path without themselves assuming responsibility for administering the country. At the All-Russian Conference of Soviets held in April, the Menshevik Irakli Tsereteli said: "There is at present no party in Russia willing to assume responsibility for governing." To which Lenin from his seat shouted, "There is!" Indeed, no other party was prepared to stake that claim. This hunger for power more than compensated for the relatively small following of the Bolsheviks.

Another advantage of Lenin's derived from the fact that he did not care about Russia. He cared about Germany and England in the sense that, for him, as a revolutionary, they were the key countries. Russia he viewed as nothing more than a stepping-stone to global upheaval; a backward country, populated mainly by an uncouth rural "petty bourgeoisie" in the shape of self-sufficient "middle" peasants and "kulaks." Such a country could not make a world revolution: at best, it could serve as a spark that would set off the powder-keg abroad. In his view, Russia was the weak link in the chain of world imperialism, the snapping of which would unleash upheavals in the heart of Europe. It was a profound personal tragedy for him that his expectations in this respect were not met and the revolution remained confined to Russia and her colonies.

Because he did not care about his country, Lenin was prepared to promise everybody whatever they wanted without giving much thought to the future. The peasants want private land for their communes? Let them take it: eventually all the land will be confiscated and collectivized anyway. Until then, "looting the loot" will win over, or at least neutralize, the peasantry. The workers demand to run the factories? Even though "workers' control" is a detestable syndico-anarchist slogan, there is no harm in granting their desires — for the time being. Once industries have been nationalized and subjected to a general economic plan of production, "workers' control" will vanish of itself. The soldiers clamour for peace? Give them peace; when the "proletarian dictatorship" is firmly in power, they will be duly mobilized for the global civil war. The national minorities call for independence? By all means: they only have to ask. The "right of national self-determination," including separate statehood, is guaranteed, with the tacit understanding that, if exercised, it will be overruled by the superior right of "proletarian self-determination." This purely tactical approach to all political problems was an enormous boon because no other party in Russia was prepared to engage in such demagoguery. Of course, when the promissory notes were presented for payment later on, Lenin had to default, alienating all those who, passively or actively, had helped him come to power and forcing him to install a totalitarian regime, which had not been his intention.

And, finally, Lenin was uniquely unscrupulous: he was prepared to collaborate on a tactical basis with absolutely anybody who served his interests, not only at home but also abroad. There is no longer any question that he took money from Imperial Germany, even while Russia and Germany were at war; we have plenty of documents dating from 1917–18 proving this fact. The Germans tried to win over similar traitors in France and England, without success. However, they succeeded beyond their wildest dreams in Russia. This was, to them, a matter of great importance because, once the Schlieffen Plan had failed, Germany desperately needed to knock Russia out of the war in order to concentrate all her forces on the Western Front. It was her one remaining hope of winning the war against a grand alliance of democratic countries with vastly superior human and material resources. Lenin, the only European socialist leader openly to call for his country's defeat, found collaboration with Germany mutually advantageous. He accepted sizeable sums of money after his return to Russia to restart his shattered party organizations and revive his suppressed press. No other group in Russia was prepared to consort with the enemy, and, therefore, none could compete with him effectively once the struggle for power got under way.

German subsidies did not stop in October 1917. They continued well into 1918, almost to the moment of Germany's capitulation. In June 1918, the Russian embassy in Moscow wired Berlin that, to keep the Bolsheviks in power, it needed three million marks a month: the sum was allocated and used to bribe Latvian and other pro-Bolshevik and neutral forces. I found in the former Central Party Archive a revealing document that had been carefully concealed for over seventy years. It is a cable from Lenin to his ambassador in Berne, Ia. Berzin, dated August 1918, instructing him to spare no expense in spreading Communist propaganda in the West: "The Berliners will send more money," he assured him; "if the scum delays, complain to me *formally*."

The Provisional Government foundered quickly, just as Nicholas II had foretold. The tsar had refused to transfer more authority to the Duma, not because he enjoyed power — he hated all ceremony — but because he believed that the politicians running it were not capable of governing; they were intellectuals used to debating and legislating but lacking any administrative experience. Indeed, as it turned out, the political stance of the Provisional Government, and its partner, the Petrograd Soviet, was replete with contradictions. Thus, for example, the Soviet pronounced the war imperialistic, while, in the same breath, insisting that it be pursued until victory. Even an illiterate worker or soldier could understand that this made no sense. And while exhorting the country to fight, the Soviet passed all kinds of laws that subverted the war effort, notably the infamous Order Number One, which effectively deprived officers of authority over their men and politicized the armed forces.

Before the end of spring 1917, Russia was in chaos.

With his conqueror's instinct Lenin realized the incur-able weakness of the Provisional Government and felt confident that the slightest push would topple it. As it turned out, he underestimated, if not its strength, then its popularity. He tried three times — in April, June, and July — to bring it down by means of street riots. In July he nearly succeeded but inexplicably lost his nerve at the critical moment. He had the government on the run, paralysed and inoperative; power was his for the asking, yet he faltered. This blunder almost caused the destruc-tion of the Bolshevik Party, for the Minister of Justice released some of the documents at his disposal showing Lenin's dealings with the Germans. When the information reached them, the infuriated garrison troops dispersed the Bolsheviks and their supporters. Lenin had to go into hiding: for the three and a half critical months that pre-ceded the October coup, he lived in concealment — first in Russia, then in Finland, and then again in Russia. The October coup was, therefore, planned and managed by his associates, including Trotsky, who adopted a more cautious tactic, calling for physical force being concealed behind a smokescreen of Soviet pseudo-legality.

Lenin had the habit of attributing to his opponents his own qualities, that is, expecting them to do what he would do under similar circumstances. After the July putsch had failed, he was convinced Kerensky would have him and his associates arrested and shot, because that is what he, Lenin, would have done in his shoes. And even though personally he had managed to elude Kerensky's

police, he was resigned to the fact that he had been defeated and that the whole Bolshevik experiment was over and
done with. He was quite unemotional in his assessment.
He settled with Zinoviev, his loyal follower, across the
Finnish border in a field hut, and devoted his free summer
days to summing up the lessons of the failed revolution
for the benefit of future generations of revolutionaries.

But then, suddenly and unexpectedly, events began to
turn his way. And, by September, the situation was ripe
for yet another putsch attempt.

Three occurrences helped turn the situation in favour
of the Bolsheviks. One was the failure of the June 1917
offensive. Kerensky, who took over the Ministry of War
in July, thought that the best way to rally the country
behind his government was to reawaken flagging patriotic sentiments by winning an impressive military victory — just as the French revolutionary armies had done in
1792. For the lessons of the French Revolution had been
well studied by Russian radicals like Kerensky and were
never far from their mind: they observed the unfolding of
events in Russia through the prism of revolutionary
France, usually with disastrous consequences. The June
offensive in no time ran out of steam, and the Russian
army rapidly disintegrated.

The second factor which aided the Bolsheviks was the
failure of the government to convene the Constituent
Assembly, to which it had solemnly committed itself on
assuming authority in March. The assembly alone would
have given Russia a legitimate authority. Undoubtedly,

had such elections been held while the Provisional Government was still in office, the majority of the seats would have gone to the Socialist-Revolutionary Party, the Bolsheviks' rivals. Had this occurred, it would have been next to impossible for the Bolsheviks to claim that they and they alone truly represented the people. Yet the government procrastinated because it always had more urgent things to attend to. This gave invaluable ammunition to the Bolsheviks, enabling them to claim that the government feared the elections, and that only the transfer of power to the soviets — accomplished by them, the Bolsheviks — would ensure timely elections to the assembly.

The third incident, and the one which contributed most directly to the success of the October coup, was the so-called Kornilov Affair, a very complicated episode of the revolution which is grossly misrepresented in much of the historical literature. Kornilov is customarily depicted as a counter-revolutionary general set on overthrowing the democratic government and assuming dictatorial powers. This version is false: it owes its widespread acceptance to the rather unusual fact that it served the interests of two mortal enemies, the Provisional Government and the Bolsheviks. In the space available I am unable to go into the details of this incident. Suffice it to say that it resulted from a bungled intrigue on the part of Kerensky, who, feeling the ground giving way under him, wanted to regain support in the soviet and, at the same time, rid himself of a general whom he came to see as a

dangerous rival. Kornilov, whom Kerensky had appointed commander of the Russian army after the abortive
July putsch, was a rather simple-minded combat officer,
a kind of Russian George Patton, highly popular with the
troops and intensely patriotic, but lacking in political
skills. He watched with dismay the collapse of both the
state and his beloved army. Convinced that he was the
candidate of all kinds of conservative forces bent on a
military coup, Kerensky lured him into sending troops to
Petrograd to help suppress another expected Bolshevik
rising. After Kornilov had carried out his orders, Kerensky accused him of seeking to capture the capital city,
overthrow the government, and take power into his own
hands. There is no evidence of a Kornilov plot, but there
is plenty of evidence of Kerensky's duplicity. Unfortunately for him, the prime minister's conflict with the
commanding general did not restore his political fortunes. On the contrary: it handed the Bolsheviks a superb
argument that a counter-revolution was indeed brewing,
and alienated from Kerensky the armed forces, which
alone could save him, as they did in July, from another
Bolshevik attempt. In October, when he sought the
army's help against the putschists, it would turn a deaf
ear to his pleas.

Although their fortunes had dramatically improved
in September 1917, most Bolsheviks, with memories of
the July débâcle fresh in mind, still hesitated to act. They
did well in soviet elections that month, campaigning on
the slogan "all power to the soviets." But they remained

Lenin, well aware that he could not win a majority, wanted to be in control before the nation had expressed its will.

His colleagues demurred. They felt that time was on the Bolsheviks' side, whereas another fiasco like the July putsch would finish them off for good. They preferred to act in a pseudo-legal fashion by convening a Congress of Soviets to assume power, but only one representing those soviets in which their party had majorities. I say "pseudo-legal" because the Bolsheviks, like any party, had no authority to convene a national congress of soviets: this was the exclusive prerogative of the Central Executive Committee of the soviets, dominated by Socialists-Revolutionaries and Mensheviks. But Russians never had much respect for legal niceties, and even less so in the turmoil of revolution and incipient civil war. Lenin rejected this strategy. He did not trust even an illegally convened soviet congress packed with his adherents to hand him power. To wait for such a congress was sheer idiocy, or treason, he wrote. No revolution waited for majorities. Hold your congress, if you insist, but first seize power and then present it with a *fait accompli*.

When the party's Central Committee met in secret session during the night of October 10, Lenin slipped into town to take part in its deliberations. He insisted that the putsch be carried out immediately. Kamenev and Zinoviev opposed this proposal most resolutely, but the others also had doubts. Subsequently, Kamenev gave an interview to a Menshevik newspaper in which he

in a minority nationwide. The armed forces, in p
lar, even though they had no more heart for fi
disliked the Bolsheviks, viewing them as a party o
coats. The peasantry stood loyally behind the Soc
Revolutionaries. Nevertheless, Lenin's instinct to l
the time to strike again was fast approaching. Fr
hideaway he badgered his associates to move
Provisional Government was weak, he insisted;
lack the courage to resist. On one occasion he wrot
if the Bolsheviks promised the soldiers immediate
and the peasants land, they would win them ov
"establish a government that *no one* will overt
When one reads these letters of Lenin, four altoge
they were not intended for publication and were
public only years later — one becomes aware ho
Lenin trusted in the forces of history. Unless the l
viks struck promptly, victory would elude the
delay is death," he wrote. To a historian not blin
faith in "historical inevitability," Lenin's exhor
emphasize to what extent October 1917 was a c
ed risk. For, if it was inevitable, what difference
make whether one struck immediately rather than
Yet it mattered enormously. Lenin was afraid t
might end or that the Provisional Government
abandon Petrograd to the Germans. He also fear
the government would pre-empt him by holding el
to the Constituent Assembly. Indeed, the gove
announced in August that the elections for th
stituent Assembly would take place in Novemb

revealed this disagreement. Lenin, in white fury, called him and Zinoviev traitors to the revolution. With these words he demonstrated that what he was planning was not a revolution. For how can one "betray" a revolution? Can one imagine anybody being accused of betraying the French Revolution? *A coup d'état*, on the other hand, can indeed be betrayed.

The minutes of the Central Committee meeting for October 10, published by the Communists in 1927, are silent about the decision to carry out the putsch which took place two weeks later. Even though other subjects were amply discussed, reference to the most important matter of all is missing. I had assumed that it had been deliberately deleted by the editors in order to maintain the fiction that October's was a popular revolution, and said so in *The Russian Revolution*. However, in 1992, I had a chance to see the original handwritten protocols of the October 10–11 meeting. The information was missing there as well. The reason for the omission could only have been Lenin's obsessive secretiveness and the fear that, if committed to paper, the information would leak out, jeopardizing the whole risky undertaking. Of course, we do not need documentary evidence to know what resolutions were adopted, for we know what followed. The Bolshevik tactic was to goad the government, by all kinds of provocative moves, into active measures against themselves, and then to claim that a counter-revolution was under way. In the alleged defence of the revolution against its alleged enemies, the Bolsheviks would seize power by occupying strategic points throughout the capital city. This was to occur during the night preceding the opening session of the Second Congress of Soviets scheduled for October 25. The next day the Congress would ratify the abolition of the Provisional Government and the transfer of all power to the soviets. The battle plan adopted was a compromise between Lenin's proposal of immediate power seizure and his associates' preference for legal camouflage.

The manner in which this strategy was implemented holds considerable interest because the combination of deception, surgically employed force, and sham legality provided a model that more than one totalitarian leader would subsequently emulate. The event which helped the Bolsheviks to set their plan in motion was an anticipated German attack on the city of Petrograd. In the second week of October, the Germans seized from the Russians several islands in the Gulf of Riga. It was widely believed that this naval operation was preparatory to an assault on Petrograd. Kerensky, acting on the advice of his military, contemplated moving the capital to Moscow. The Socialists in the Soviet reacted with the usual combination of paranoia and hysteria. Accusing the government of wanting to abandon "Red Petrograd" to the enemy, they proposed creating a Soviet military force capable of defending the city from the expected German attack. The Bolsheviks at first opposed this motion because they thought it would strengthen the Provisional Government, but then they reversed themselves and supported it, for they came to realize that the only force which the soviet could count on were their own armed units, directed by their military organization, and that it would provide a perfect Soviet fig-leaf for their coup. In agreeing to what had been a Menshevik motion, they only added the proviso that the soviet's "Military-Revolutionary Committee," as it was designated, protect Petrograd also from domestic "counter-revolutionaries," which they understood to mean the Provisional Government. With Menshevik and Socialist-Revolutionary help, they now acquired a mechanism for taking power; for the Military-Revolutionary Committee, or Milrevkom, was nothing but a front for their own military organization. It probably was no accident that the meeting of the Bolshevik Central Committee which decided on the power seizure took place one day after the Soviet had voted to create the Milrevkom.

During the two weeks which preceded the projected coup, acting with the tacit consent of the Soviet, the Bolsheviks sent commissars to all the military units stationed in Petrograd and vicinity, instructing them to ignore orders from the government unless countersigned by the Military-Revolutionary Committee. It seems that no one objected to this manoeuvre, which undermined the government's authority over its troops and transferred them into the hands of Lenin's lieutenants. It had the effect of neutralizing the garrison, 240,000 men strong, the only force capable of thwarting Bolshevik designs.

The world-shaking events that took place on the night

of October 24 were anti-climactic: how often happenings labelled "historical" turn out be little more than empty ceremonial occasions, while those that affect destinies of millions attract, in their day, scarcely any attention! Lenin was still in hiding when the critical measures were implemented. He was an incurable coward who took cover whenever there was any risk to him personally, even as he exhorted his followers to battle. Trotsky was far more courageous and very much in evidence during these critical days, haranguing crowds, taunting the government, and helping in other ways to set the stage for the coup. So were Podvoiskii, Nevskii, and other commanders. During the night of October 24, responding to some half-hearted protective measures by the government, armed units of the Military-Revolutionary Committee took over the capital city's key installations — the post office and telegraph, the central telephone bureau, the headquarters of the government's military command. It was a bloodless coup, carried out while Petrograd was asleep and unaware of what was taking place. Government sentries guarding these installations were relieved and told to go home. The military headquarters was taken in the same manner: Bolshevik officers walked into the unguarded Mikhailovskii Palace and simply replaced those officiating there. There was no resistance. As Lenin would afterwards say, taking power in Petrograd was as easy as "picking up a feather."

The next day, only one building still remained in government hands — namely, the Winter Palace. Here huddled the ministers, defended by a battalion of women, a platoon of war invalids, a few bicyclists, and some military cadets. The building was never stormed: the much-reproduced photograph of a column of workers and Red Guards charging it is a fake, a still from Eisenstein's movie *October*, filmed in 1927 with the help of extras. Several attempts to storm the palace were made, but as soon as they ran into fire, the attackers retreated. Eventually the women, the bicyclists, and the invalids left the Winter Palace because Kerensky, who had gone to the front in a borrowed American car to get assistance, was nowhere in sight. When most of the defenders had departed, the attackers climbed through the open windows and back doors. They were not opposed because the ministers told the cadets, who remained to the end, prepared to fight, that they wanted no bloodshed. The ministers meekly surrendered and the putsch was over.

Still, Lenin was his usual cautious self. He took power, not on behalf of the Bolshevik Party — the words "Bolshevik Party" do not appear anywhere in the early documents — but on behalf of the soviet. And he intimated that he wanted to have a democratic transitional government; the word "socialism" does not appear in the announcement proclaiming the overthrow of the Provisional Government which he drafted in the early hours of October 25. He had originally written "*Da zdravstvuet sotsializm!*" ("Long live socialism!"), but then had second thoughts and crossed these words out because he did not want to alarm anybody. Hence, no one had any idea that anything of importance had transpired: it seemed merely a shift from dual power to unitary power under which the stronger partner, the soviet, assumed full responsibility. The next day the cafés were filled, the opera reopened, and life returned to normal. It seemed to be just another one of those government crises that had been occurring with increasing frequency since the tsar had abdicated. The Bolsheviks contributed to this perception by calling theirs also "Provisional Government." It was widely believed that as soon as the Constituent Assembly had met, the Bolshevik government would gracefully yield power. And the new masters did nothing to dispel this mirage.

The Bolsheviks did hold elections to the Constituent Assembly, but when it transpired that they gained only 24 per cent of the vote and that the new government would be run by the Socialists-Revolutionaries, they dispersed the assembly. Afterward, they dropped the adjective "provisional" from the title of their government and set themselves up as a one-party regime, which, except for a few months in early 1918, when they gave a splinter Socialist-Revolutionary group several commissar portfolios, was open exclusively to members of the Bolshevik Party.

In perpetrating these outrages, the Bolsheviks were enormously aided by the illusions and the fears of the democratic socialists, who between them had garnered nearly three-quarters of the national vote and, on the face of it, enjoyed massive popular backing, had they chosen to act. The socialists knew well what the Bolsheviks were up to; that, in spite of their democratic professions, they were planning to establish a one-party dictatorship. But they were inhibited from acting by the fear that any attempt to liquidate the Bolsheviks coup would lead to the destruction of the socialist movement as a whole and the triumph of the counter-revolution. At the time of the Bolshevik take-over, the Menshevik paper *Novaia zhizn'* wrote:

> It is essential above all to take into account the tragic fact that any violent liquidation of the Bolshevik coup will, at the same time, result inevitably in the liquidation of all the conquests of the Russian Revolution.

Throughout the revolution and civil war, the Mensheviks and the Socialists-Revolutionaries criticized the Bolsheviks, but at all critical moments they supported them against their opponents. This was particularly the case in 1919, when they sided with the Reds against the Whites and sabotaged the anti-Bolshevik armed struggle. More than once, when the workers and soldiers would come to them and offer to resist the Bolsheviks, the Socialists-Revolutionaries and Mensheviks would refuse them support on the grounds that such resistance would help the forces of reaction. They further justified their unwillingness to confront the new regime on any other but the verbal level with the argument that time was working for democracy because, being a minority party facing unprecedented problems of creating a socialist society, the Bolsheviks would have no choice but sooner or later to invite them into government. Thus motivated, they ended up utterly passive. And, in the end, except for those who emigrated, they all perished.

This cursory survey indicates that what occurred in October 1917 was a classical modern *coup d'état* accomplished without mass support. It was a surreptitious seizure of the nerve centres of the modern state, carried out under false slogans in order to neutralize the population at large, the true purpose of which was revealed only after the new claimants to power were firmly in the saddle. Curzio Malaparte, in his book *Coup d'État: The Technique of Revolution* (New York, 1932), on the mechanics of the modern seizure of power, based his analyses very much on what happened in Russia; then he also witnessed a similar process in Italy under Mussolini and drew parallels.

The population at large offered little resistance at a time when such resistance would have made all the difference because it believed that the new regime could not last. The so-called Soviet government was seen as made up of crazy utopians who would be swept from the scene as suddenly as they had appeared. When Bolshevik policies began to affect adversely the interests of workers and peasants — the former through the liquidation of "worker control" and independent trade unions, the latter through ruthless food exactions — they rebelled. The years 1920–1 witnessed massive resistance to the new regime. As the historian Vladimir Brovkin has demonstrated, the true civil war started only after the White armies had been crushed. It was a war pitting millions of peasants against millions of Red Army troops, in which hundreds of thousands perished. But by then it was too late. The mutinous sailors of Kronshtadt, the striking workers of Petrograd, and the peasant partisans of Tambov or Siberia had no more chance of defeating the government than, in tsarist days, the rebels led by Stepan Razin or Emelian Pugachev.

Still, the acquisition of power in this manner had its own logic, of which the Bolsheviks were only dimly aware. By imposing on the country minority rule and refusing to consider yielding or even sharing power, they laid the foundations of totalitarianism. Lenin had genuinely believed that, once the "counter-revolution" had been smashed, popular democracy would triumph. But when the "counter-revolution" turned out to be not only a relatively thin layer of dispossessed landowners, bourgeois, and officials, but the great majority of the nation, as long as he was unwilling to give up power, he had no choice but to resort to an exceedingly repressive regime. His erratic behaviour in 1921 and 1922 can be in large measure explained by the dismay he felt at so many things going wrong: as he once put it, the driver steers the car in one direction and the car goes "God knows where." Because he refused to surrender the steering-wheel, he willy-nilly created conditions which made inevitable the rise to power of a personal dictator, who turned out to be even more ruthless than he.

CHAPTER THREE:

Why Did Stalin Succeed Lenin?

As I HAVE REMARKED previously, the collapse of tsarism, while not improbable, was certainly not inevitable. As for the Bolshevik triumph in October 1917, as Lenin foresaw, it was a rather chancy affair: it required various mistakes of their opponents for the Bolsheviks to win power and hold on to it. At the time, it seemed more likely that post-tsarist Russia would be governed by a coalition of conservative generals and politicians than by the Communists. As for the third "why" of the Russian Revolution — why did Stalin succeed Lenin? — here I am inclined to have recourse to the notion of inevitability. It is my view that once the Soviet regime was in place and

Lenin pursued his visionary program without regard to the almost universal opposition it aroused, when he had fallen seriously ill, the apparatus which he had created naturally rallied around Stalin, the most competent and popular Communist politician. This contention puts me at odds with much of the revisionist school of Russian historians, whose adherents, while insisting on the inevitability of tsarism's collapse and Bolshevism's triumph, treat the rise of Stalin as an inexplicable accident. I have yet to see a satisfactory Marxist explanation why history, after the death of Lenin, took a thirty-year detour by vesting what Lenin himself had called "unbounded power" in a despot whom the revisionists regard as a traitor to the cause of Leninism. In particular, they do not address the question of why, if, as they claim, Lenin in 1917 enjoyed widespread support, his regime had to resort from the beginning to dictatorial methods, and why these methods, conceivably justifiable as emergency measures, became a permanent feature of the Communist system.

One often hears it said that Stalin hijacked the revolution and that, in the normal course of events, power should have passed to Trotsky, or perhaps Bukharin. Although each has his partisans among historians, neither Trotsky nor Bukharin had the slightest chance of being selected by Lenin to succeed him: we learn from archival sources that Lenin dismissed Trotsky as "having not a clue about politics" and explicitly demanded that Bukharin be kept out of politics. When one studies without preconceptions the sources of the period, one is inex- orably driven to the conclusion that Stalin was far in front in the competition for Lenin's post, possibly as early as 1920 but certainly by 1922. Stalinism had three prin- cipal causes: 1/ the failure of the Bolsheviks in 1919–20 to export the revolution to the industrial West; 2/ the immense responsibilities of administering every aspect of Soviet life which the Communist Party assumed, one con- sequence of which was the emergence of a correspond- ingly immense party bureaucracy; and 3/ the rise of an opposition to being ruled by intellectuals among workers, allegedly the principal constituency of the Communist Party. But as I will indicate, personalities, too, played their part.

Let me begin with the failure to export the revolu- tion. As I have explained before, the Bolsheviks took power in Russia by chance. It so happened that Russia had a weak government, one unable, not always for rea- sons of its own making, to cope with the strains of a war of attrition. It collapsed in the midst of war while every other belligerent government managed to hang on. The Bolsheviks seized power in Russia because it had become available for a power seizure. Were the choice up to them, they would much rather have taken over Germany or England. But once fate determined that they were masters of Russia, they had to export revolution to the industrial West. They regarded Russia as a backward peas- ant country with a small and backward working class. They feared — and said so on more than one occasion —

that, unless they carried the revolution to western Europe, she would slide back and communism would drown in the morass of petty-bourgeois peasant culture.

For this reason, it was vital as quickly as possible to carry the revolution to the West, where, the Bolsheviks believed, lived a numerous and truly class-conscious proletariat. For all their vaunted realism, they were remarkably naïve about the revolutionary potential of the West European working class. They did not realize, and refused to be instructed by foreign Communists, that the European worker respected private property, and that, as a beneficiary of valuable social-welfare programs, had no interest in overthrowing the state. They treated such advice as an excuse for inaction. They were so beholden to wishful thinking that they interpreted every trouble in the West as the onset of a revolution. The Bolshevik press of 1918–20 was filled with headlines announcing "Revolution in Finland," "Revolution in France," "Revolution in Italy." Every strike, every protest demonstration, every cabinet crisis was hailed as a portent of imminent collapse. Lenin hoped to unleash a European civil war while the world war was still in progress. With the meager personnel and financial means at his disposal, he promoted mutinies in the armed forces and strikes among workers in both the Allied camp and the countries of the Central Powers. Success eluded him because foreign governments were sufficiently alert to cope with such subversion. But once the war ended, seemingly unlimited prospects opened up, especially among the defeated and demoralized anti-Allied powers. In the winter of 1918–19, immediately after the fall of the Kaiser's government, Moscow pushed the pro-Communist Spartacus League into open rebellion. In March 1919, it founded the Communist International to organize worldwide revolutionary movements. Agents of the Comintern were busy everywhere: now in Iran and Turkey, now in Hungary and Austria, and repeatedly in Germany. But, once again, success eluded them. Not a single country in Europe was revolutionized. Communism came to Europe — at any rate, to its eastern half — only in the wake of the Second World War, carried on Soviet tanks.

The height of expectations for a European revolution occurred in the summer of 1920, during the war with Poland. The origins and course of this war — rightly called one of the most decisive in all history — are even today not entirely clear. After studying as many relevant documents as are presently available, I have concluded that each of the belligerent parties, the Poles and the Russians, prepared to attack without realizing that the other was making similar preparations. Joseph Pilsudski, the head of the new Polish state, who in October 1919, in the decisive phase of the Russian Civil War, had helped the Reds defeat the Whites because he judged them a lesser danger to his country, formulated a long-term strategy. He believed that the day would inevitably come when Germany and Russia would rise again and join hands to crush Poland. To prevent such a catastrophe, he decided to create a chain of buffer states separating Poland from

Russia. He envisaged the Baltic states, Belorussia, and even the Caucasian republics as part of that buffer, with Ukraine as its linchpin. He came to terms with the Ukrainian national leader Simon Petlura with the view of helping him expel the Communists from the Ukraine, which they had recently conquered, and establishing an independent Ukrainian republic allied with Poland. When he attacked the Soviet Ukraine in April 1920, Pilsudski had no intention of overthrowing the Communist regime in Russia: his objective was a limited one — namely, helping set up a sovereign, pro-Polish Ukrainian state.

There are bits and pieces of evidence that the Bolsheviks, for their own reasons, were preparing to attack Poland at about the same time. I do not believe that the Red Army knew that the Poles were about to invade; nor did the Poles know that the Red Army was making preparations to attack them. Much of the information on these preparations is still concealed in Russian archives. But a coded cable of February 1920, sent by Lenin to Stalin, who at the time was with the Revolutionary-Military Council at the Southern Front, reveals a great deal. In it, Lenin asked what measures Stalin was proposing to create a "striking force" (*udarnyi kulak*) against Polish Galicia. There are other facts indicative of offensive plans. They had to do with developments in western and southern Europe, where Lenin, in his feverish imagination, perceived massive revolutionary movements on the verge of explosion and in need of Soviet military help. As I will indicate below, to Lenin the recent victory over the Whites served as a signal for the Red Army to go on the offensive against the West.

The Poles struck first. They marched on Kiev, occupied it in early May 1920, but soon found themselves stopped in their tracks and then thrown back. The Ukrainian national uprising on which they had counted never occurred; instead, much of Russia, especially her conservative, nationalistic elements, rallied behind the Communist regime as the defender of the nation's "patrimony." The Poles were quickly expelled, and then the question arose: should the Red Army advance into ethnic Poland? Trotsky opposed such a move: the British were warning Moscow that if it crossed the so-called Curzon Line separating ethnic Russians and Ukrainians from the Poles, they would intervene on Poland's behalf. But Lenin decided to gamble. The moment had come, he believed, to march on Europe. The Russian archives have recently disgorged a secret speech of his, delivered in September 1920, after the defeat of the Red Army in Poland, which sheds much light on these events. Of all the archival materials I have seen, it is perhaps the most revealing. In an unusually rambling speech, even for a man given to making rambling speeches, Lenin said that, after the defeat of the White Armies, which in his eyes were merely hirelings of the Western Allies, the Politburo decided that the defensive phase of the conflict with capitalism was over: the Communist side had won. The time had come to go on the offensive. Both Germany and England were seething with social unrest. He attached particular importance to the emergence in England of the Council of Action, an organization formed in mid-August 1920 by the Trade Union Congress and the Labour Party, to carry out a general strike if the British government attempted to give military aid to Poland. In his ignorance of English conditions, Lenin actually believed that the Council of Action was a counterpart of the Russian soviets, and that, in the summer of 1920, England was in the same situation in which Russia had been in February 1917. He spoke of "hundreds of thousands" of German communists marching to join the Red Army advancing into Poland. He also saw revolution imminent in southern Europe. In another cable to Stalin from July 1920, he wrote that "the time has come to exacerbate the revolution in Italy, and en route [to] sovietize Hungary, Czechoslovakia, and Romania as well."

The Soviet débâcle in Poland appears to have been due to overconfidence. Trotsky subsequently blamed it on Stalin, insisting that Stalin, as political commissar with the southern army which had moved into Galicia, disobeyed orders to have the southern army link up with Tukhachevskii, who was laying siege to Warsaw. But judging by Lenin's cable, it seems more likely that Stalin's mission was to invade the southern parts of Central Europe and Italy. I think Lenin decided that Warsaw was his for the asking, and that his army should pursue broader strategic objectives. This misconception led him to commit another fatal blunder. He ordered Tukhachevskii to detach major forces, including a cavalry corps, from the army besieging Warsaw, and send them into Pomerania. He apparently did this for two reasons: to link up with the imaginary hordes of German Communists streaming eastward, and to win the support of the German nationalists by turning over to them the Polish corridor and reuniting East Prussia with Germany proper. Leaving Stalin in the south and ordering Tukhachevskii to advance into Pomerania before Poland had been crushed was what made possible the "Miracle on the Vistula." Incidentally, contrary to widespread misperceptions, credit for the Polish victory does not belong to the French, whose military mission the Poles isolated and whose strategic advice they ignored.

The defeat in Poland had a shattering effect on Lenin. Confident of his revolutionary intuition and experience, he had ordered the Red Army and the so-called Polrevkom, the Polish Revolutionary Committee which was to set up a Polish soviet government, to advance the same slogans which had been successfully employed in Russia: seize the land, take over factories, hang the kulaks and the bourgeois. But in Poland these slogans did not resonate. Lenin afterwards complained to Clara Zetkin, the German communist, that the Polish peasants and workers did not help the Red Army, but defended the *pany*, their Polish lords, capturing and killing the brave Russian lads sent to liberate them. He had run into something that he had not anticipated, a very different political culture from the one prevailing in his own country: a culture that respected property and responded to patriotic appeals. Trotsky told Chiang Kai-shek, the head of the Kuomintang, which at the time had close relations with Moscow, that, after the débâcle in Poland, Lenin had given orders never again to use the Red Army in direct operations abroad in order not to run afoul of nationalism.

By 1921 it had become clear to all but the most incorrigible optimists that there would be no repetition of October 1917 anywhere else and that for an indeterminate period the revolution would remain confined to Russia and her possessions. The concept of "socialism in one country" was not launched by Stalin in his conflict with Trotsky, but earlier, by Lenin himself.

Now this change of course carried certain inexorable implications which Lenin articulated and Stalin subsequently acted on. Lenin, it seems, decided that just as communism had triumphed in Russia following one world war, so it would triumph globally only after another world war. Of course, one should exploit every revolutionary situation abroad as it presented itself, but in the main rely on building in Soviet Russia an invincible modern fighting machine in preparation for such a global conflict. Diplomatically, every means should be used to exacerbate relations between Germany and the Allied powers. In 1921, Lenin and Trotsky established clandestine military cooperation with the German Reichswehr, offering it an opportunity to circumvent the limitations which the Versailles Treaty had imposed on it by offering facilities for the manufacture and testing of the forbidden weapons (tanks, planes, submarines, and poison gas) on Soviet territory. In exchange, the Germans undertook to instruct the Russians in the most up-to-date military strategy and tactics. This collaboration, which lasted until the fall of 1933 and contributed greatly to the modernization of both Soviet and German armies, is only now, with the opening of Russian archives, becoming better known because the Germans had destroyed much of the relevant documentation.

Preventing a rapprochement among Germany, France, and England became a major objective of Soviet diplomacy in 1920–1 and afterwards. In the archives I found a remarkable instruction from Lenin to the Commissar of Foreign Affairs, George Chicherin, dating from early 1922 as preparations got under way for the Genoa Conference. The purpose of this conference, convened by the Allies, was to settle outstanding financial and other problems dividing them from both Germany and Russia and to reintegrate them into the international community. It is common knowledge that the Genoa Conference was wrecked by the separate treaty signed by Germany and Russia in Rapallo, in which their differences were bilaterally resolved. Not previously known was that Lenin had deliberately sabotaged the conference, apparently from fear of a rapprochement between Germany and her one-time enemies. He wrote to Chicherin, who was to head the Soviet delegation in Genoa: "It suits us that Genoa be wrecked . . . but *not by us*, of course." He asked him to devise a means of so doing and to return the note so that it could be burned. It fortunately survived, casting additional light on the disruptive tactics of Soviet diplomacy in the postwar world.

The collapse of efforts to export revolution meant that one had to build a stable state and a professional bureaucracy to administer it. The task required very different personalities from those who had spent most of their adult lives in the revolutionary underground. Indeed, the very rules of the Bolshevik Party ensured that its members would have no competence other than making revolution since it demanded of them full-time dedication to revolutionary activity. Lenin's associates were not capable of running a regular, ordinary state, of dealing with the mountains of paperwork, of giving instructions to the scattered party cells, of appointing low-level officials — they found such routine insufferably tedious. Stalin was the only high-ranking Bolshevik who cared about such matters and showed a talent for them. That was a critical factor in his rise to power.

Next, let me turn to the bureaucracy. The bureaucracy grew enormously because, under communism, everything that involved two or more people had to be, without exception, directed by party organs. The entire national economy, previously mostly in private hands, was now managed from the centre: so were all social institutions, cultural associations, the clergy, everything down to the smallest entities because, as seasoned revolutionaries, the

Bolsheviks knew well that the most harmless-looking organization can serve as a front for political activity. This meant a mammoth bureaucracy. Since the Communist cadres were far from adequate for such responsibilities, whether viewed in terms of numbers or of skills, the regime had to hire so-called bourgeois specialists. These implicit class enemies had to be as closely supervised as the "bourgeois military specialists" had been during the Civil War. This requirement entailed a vast increase in the size and responsibilities of the political police, which, from the early 1920s on, insinuated itself into every aspect of Soviet life.

Stalin realized early that he could build up a powerful bureaucratic apparatus loyal to him personally by means of material rewards. In April 1922, Lenin had him appointed General Secretary. I will explain later on why this happened. Using this office, Stalin promptly began to lavish favours on the top bureaucracy of the Communist Party, headquartered in Moscow. He provided key *apparatchiks* with better living quarters, supplementary food rations, trips to Western sanatoria, and so on. By the time Lenin had to start withdrawing, for reasons of health, from the day-to-day management of the party and state, Soviet Russia had a privileged caste of party officials numbering between fifteen and twenty-five thousand, a large proportion of them appointed by Stalin's machine. This group, residing in Moscow, became increasingly independent of the masses of Communist Party members numbering in the hundreds of thousands, whom it deprived of any voice in running party affairs, not only in the country at large, but also in their own bailiwicks.

Lenin was only vaguely aware of these developments. In *State and Revolution*, which he wrote in 1917, he had predicted that, under communism, there would be no bureaucracy: any ordinary cook would rule, and soon everyone would become accustomed to nobody ruling. In January 1919, in an exchange with the Menshevik historian N.A. Rozhkov, he wrote that Rozhkov's proposition that he assume dictatorial powers to solve the food crisis was "nonsense" because the apparatus had become too large for any one person to run it. When, in 1922, Trotsky alerted him to the fact that the party apparatus absorbed tens of millions of gold rubles, Lenin was beside himself with astonishment and anger. He resorted to a purge to rid the party of opportunists and idlers, but it made little difference. In the last months of his conscious life, he became obsessed with the question of bureaucracy, thinking up ever new schemes to reduce and improve it. To no avail. The all-powerful party–state dictatorship which he had imposed on Russia became beholden to its own servants.

The third factor accounting for the triumph of Stalin was the emergence of resistance to the communist system within the working class. At the Ninth Party Congress, which met in the spring of 1920, and then again at the Tenth Congress the following year, the worker members of the party voiced serious objections to the way the party was run. They said it was being bureaucratized and that the bureaucracy was controlled by intellectuals: in Russian *beloruchki* — "white hands" — people who had never worked manually and quickly acquired the habits of tsarist state functionaries. This had to change radically. Every party official ought to be required to spend at least three months a year doing physical labour, either in agriculture or in industry. Gradually, as worker cadres were trained, the management of the nation's economy should be entrusted to the trade unions. These demands were made by the oldest worker members of the Bolshevik Party, whose party affiliation antedated 1917, and even 1905.

Lenin was appalled. He had always hated what he called "spontaneity" and we would call "democracy." He never believed, either before or after the revolution, that workers were capable either of producing socialism or of running the economy. In his exasperation he began now to attack the Russian working class itself. In an address to the Eleventh Party Congress (1922), he made the astonishing statement that Russia had no proletariat in the Marxist sense, but all kinds of malingerers who took factory jobs to avoid army service. At that point, Alexander Shliapnikov, the leading Bolshevik of worker origin and the head of what came to be known as the "Workers' Opposition," had the courage publicly to congratulate Lenin on being in the "vanguard of a nonexistent class." In due course, he paid with his life for such remarks.

Lenin now became seriously worried about the future of the party. The rise of an opposition within party ranks (outside these ranks, it had been effectively snuffed out) presented him with two alternatives. He could agree to democratize the party, to give the workers and others among the loyal opposition a voice in its decision making and altogether restore to it such elements of self-rule as it had had before and during the revolution. But, mistrustful as he was of the workers' commitment to his brand of radicalism, he feared that such a concession would dilute the movement's revolutionary zeal as well as rob the party of its greatest asset, which was disciplined unity. So he settled on the other alternative, which was to outlaw all organized dissent within the party. At the Tenth Congress he had the party pass in secret a resolution banning what he called "factionalism." By this he meant any organized opposition to the course formally adopted by the party's governing organs, the Politburo and Central Committee. One of the reasons Lenin chose Stalin to serve as General Secretary was his confidence that Stalin would beat down all factionalism and maintain the party on a steady "orthodox" course. What he did not anticipate was that Stalin would depict any personal opposition to him and his methods of management then and later as "factionalism." This ruling destroyed the last vestiges of democracy in the Communist Party.

Trotsky voted for this resolution, which became public knowledge a year later, and he soon found himself victimized by its terms. Every time he attempted to get together a group of like-minded individuals to steer the party on a different course or to stand up to Stalin, he would be accused of "factionalism." And he could hardly fight back because he himself had declared that "the party was always right." This meant, implicitly, that whoever controlled the party was always right as well. And it so happened that this person was not he but his bitterest enemy.

Stalin increasingly used his post to place loyal people in positions of responsibility. This became easier after Moscow had abandoned the practice of having provincial party secretaries — the *gubernatory* of the new regime — chosen by the provincial cells. By 1922–3 they were all appointed from the centre. Why? The justification was that functionaries elected locally were not sufficiently aware of broader issues, thinking in purely parochial terms. Hence, the Moscow centre argued, it had no choice but to send to the provinces administrators with a national and international perspective on things. These appointments, a form of patronage, were made by Stalin, the only person to belong to all three leading organizations of the party: the Politburo, which decided on matters of policy; the Orgburo, which dealt with personnel matters; and the Secretariat, which controlled the flow of paper. Trotsky belonged only to one of them, the Politburo. So Stalin was in an unrivalled position, which assured his future career for some time before Lenin's death.

Finally there is the intangible personality factor.

Fellow-travellers and Communists who believe in communism with a human face have gone to great lengths since 1953 to depict Stalin as a man who had perverted Lenin and Leninism and seized power while Lenin was not looking. Trotsky contributed to this myth with all kinds of lies and half-truths about his and Stalin's relationship with Lenin. His version of events was reinforced by Deutscher's three-volume adulatory biography of Trotsky [*The Prophet Armed: Trotsky: 1879–1921*, New York, 1954; *The Prophet Unarmed: Trotsky: 1921–1929*, New York, 1959; and *The Prophet Outcast: Trotsky: 1929–1940*, New York, 1963] which rests on very shaky documentary evidence. There are strong indications, however, that, except for the last four months of Lenin's conscious life, prior to March 1923, when he had the final debilitating stroke and lost the power of speech, Lenin was close to Stalin, relied on his judgment, and entrusted him with ever greater responsibilities. At the same time there are no indications in the sources that he ever cared personally for Trotsky. He admired him and valued his contributions, for which reason he resisted efforts by Stalin's minions, Zinoviev and Kamenev, to have Trotsky expelled. But he was not close to him.

Trotsky was never popular with the Bolshevik Old Guard, even at the height of his fame, when he headed the Red Army. He had joined the party late, in July 1917, barely three months before the October putsch. During the preceding fifteen years he had attacked Lenin and his followers in the acerbic manner which Russian radical circles regarded as *bon ton*. This background earned him the reputation for being an opportunist. In addition, he was not a team player and refused, on one occasion, a post that was offered to him by Lenin. In 1922, Lenin, feeling ill and looking for help, wanted him as one of his four deputies. I have seen the document with the Politburo resolution to this effect: every member agreed, except Trotsky who "categorically refused." This kind of wilful insubordination in a party that treated its members as soldiers was unprecedented and unforgivable. Trotsky reacted in this manner because he felt that the post offered to him was beneath his dignity, which did not prevent him later on from making it appear as if Lenin had appointed him his successor. Trotsky was also gruff and arrogant. The archives contain the results of the election to the Central Committee held at the Tenth Party Congress in 1921, one year before Stalin assumed the post of General Secretary. They indicate that Trotsky came in tenth, far below Stalin, and even after Molotov.

Last but not least, the factor which prevented Trotsky from succeeding Lenin was his Jewishness. Trotsky hated to be reminded that he was a Jew. Whenever anybody came to him asking him to help other Jews, he would explode in anger and insist that he was not a Jew but an "internationalist." On one occasion he said that the fate of the Jews concerned him as little as the fate of the Bulgarians. He was in the Ukraine in 1919 during the horrible pogroms carried out by White and independent Cossack bands. Not once did he do anything about them, even when he could, as in 1920, when the Red Cavalry retreating from Poland massacred Jews. In October 1923, when he was fighting for his political life, he explained to the Central Committee Plenum that he had refused the post of deputy two years earlier because, while his Jewish origin meant nothing to him, it meant something to the country at large, and he would have supplied ammunition to the enemies of the Soviet regime who claimed that Jews were running Russia. He added that, even though Lenin pooh-poohed this argument, in his heart he knew that it was right.

All these factors made it quite impossible for Trotsky to succeed Lenin. Stalin was Trotsky's opposite. It is puzzling how different the early Stalin, during the first five years of the regime, was — or, at any rate appeared — from the later bloody tyrant. A self-effacing team-player, a jolly Georgian who would invite visitors to his *dacha* to sing, dance, and joke, he tried to be friends with everyone, even Trotsky, until Trotsky rebuffed him. He would visit Lenin more often than anyone else when Lenin lived incapacitated in Gorki. As for Trotsky, at the end of 1922, he had to ask for directions to Gorki — apparently he had never been there.

Trotsky would bombard Lenin with long memoranda, explaining why so much was wrong in Soviet Russia and how to correct it. Lenin would frequently scribble on such memoranda "*V arkhiv*" — "Into the Archive" — meaning that they required no action. Stalin, by contrast, would send him succinct notes, a few pointed sentences, suggesting to Lenin how best to implement his decisions, but never questioning the decisions themselves.

Lenin awoke to Stalin's ambitions only late, at the end of 1922, and in March 1923, shortly before he had the stroke that put him out of commission, suggested that he be replaced as General Secretary. But if one reads that famous note carefully, what does it say? Stalin is coarse, Stalin is rude, Stalin is impatient — all relatively minor vices that might be serious flaws in an administrator, but not in a human being. Lenin does not seem to have penetrated Stalin's personality and noticed the mass killer lurking in his black soul. He simply did not think he was suited for the particular job which he had entrusted to him. Throughout most of Lenin's indisposition, it was Stalin, together with Kamenev and Zinoviev, who ran the party, who did Lenin's bidding and, except on a couple of issues, such as the nationality question, saw eye to eye with Lenin.

I believe that Stalin sincerely regarded himself as a disciple of Lenin, a man destined to carry out his agenda to a successful conclusion. With one exception, the killing of fellow Communists — a crime Lenin did not commit — he faithfully implemented Lenin's domestic and foreign programs. He prevented the party from being riven by factionalism; he "liquidated" the noxious intelligentsia; he collectivized agriculture, as Lenin had desired; he subjected the Russian economy to a single plan; he industrialized Russia; he built a powerful Red Army; he collaborated with German nationalists in order to prevent the stabilization of Europe; and he helped unleash the Second World War, which had been one of Lenin's objectives as well.

Although some historians still try to contrast the "good" Lenin with the "bad" Stalin, this distinction is becoming less and less sustainable, especially now that in Russia herself it is being abandoned by all but diehard Communists.